WS

Vet

First published in the UK in 2009 by
QED Publishing
A Quarto Group company
226 City Road
London EC1V 2TT
www.qed-publishing.co.uk

A catalogue record for this book is available from
the British Library.

ISBN 978 1 84835 157 8

Printed and bound in China

Author Amanda Askew
Designer and Illustrator Andrew Crowson
Veterinary consultant Catheryn Hancock
Consultants Shirley Bickler and Tracey Dils

Publisher Steve Evans
Creative Director Zeta Davies
Managing Editor Amanda Askew

Words in bold are
explained in the
glossary on page 24.

People who help us

Vet

Amanda Askew
Andrew Crowson

QED Publishing

Meet Dr Beth.
She is a vet and
she helps sick
and hurt animals
to get better.

Dr Beth arrives at the clinic at about 8 o'clock. Clara looks after the office. She is chatting to Nurse Brown about today's **patients**.

5

Dr Beth and Nurse Brown go to the hospital first to check on the animals there.

"Barney's leg is **healing** well,"
Dr Beth tells Nurse Brown.

"Harry's tummy is looking good after the lump was taken away."

Molly the cat had kittens last week.
Some of the kittens could not **suckle**,
so they came to hospital to learn
how to feed.

"How are you feeling Molly? Your kittens are looking very well. I think you can go home today."

9

Then Dr Beth checks the appointment book to see which patients are visiting her today.

"It's going to be a busy day, Clara! Please send the first patient in."

Daisy the dog needs to have her claws cut before they get too long.

Charlie the cat has been fighting and has scratches on his leg.

Thomas the turtle
is not eating
very well. This
is because he
has just finished
hibernating.

12

Polly the puppy needs a **vaccination** to help her to stay healthy.

Rosie the rabbit's teeth are too long. Dr Beth will cut them for her.

Zuzu the snake just seems quiet.

Ronald the rat escaped from his cage and hurt his tail.

Carly the cat has fleas. She has scratched her skin and it is sore.

Dr Beth's next patient is a little more serious. Dart the dog looks very unhappy and his owner is upset.

"Dart won't eat and he has been sick."

"Let's see. Now, I'm just going to feel his tummy. Is there a chance that Dart could've eaten something that he shouldn't have?"

"He chews lots of things, but he's never eaten any of them before!"

19

Dr Beth sends Dart for an **X-ray**
with Nurse Brown, just in case.

Nurse Brown brings
the X-ray to Dr Beth.

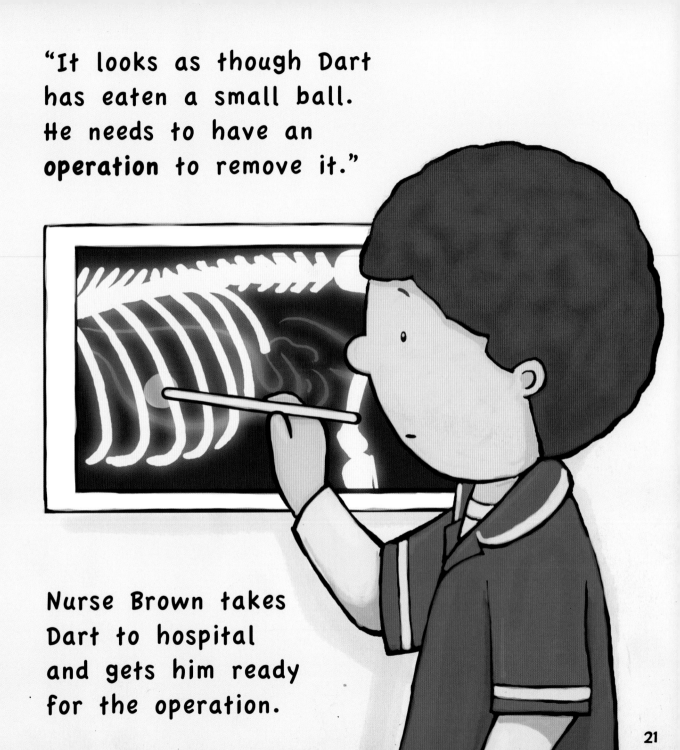

"It looks as though Dart has eaten a small ball. He needs to have an **operation** to remove it."

Nurse Brown takes Dart to hospital and gets him ready for the operation.

After an hour,
Dr Beth phones
Dart's owner.

"Dart swallowed
a ball, but he's
going to be
fine. We'll keep
him in hospital
for a couple
of days. You
can see him
tomorrow."

"Thank you so much," she says.

"No problem,"
Dr Beth smiles.

Glossary

Clinic A place where medical treatment is given.

Heal When skin or bone grows back and becomes healthy again.

Hibernate To go into a kind of deep sleep for winter.

Operation When someone's body is cut open to fix a part that is damaged.

Patient Someone who visits a doctor when they are sick.

Suckle To feed a young animal or baby with milk from its mother.

Vaccination When an animal or person is given an injection to protect them from a disease.

X-ray A photograph of the insides of something, such as bones inside the body.